The Allen Book of ~PONIES~

by Carolyn Henderson
and Jennifer Bell

British Ponies

There are still a few clues left to his origin – the ergot, at the back of the fetlock, is all that is left of eohippus's soft feet. His speed enabled him to run away from bigger, clumsier animals who were his enemies – if a pony is frightened, the first thing he will do is try to run away.

Eohippus

Ponies come in all shapes and sizes. Today there are lots of different breeds, but they all descend from an animal called eohippus that ran wild on the plains of North America 55 million years ago. He did not look anything like the modern horse or pony: he was about the size of a medium-sized dog and had soft toes on each foot. Gradually, as the world developed, he grew and changed into the horse of today.

Welsh pony breeds are prized throughout the world. The Welsh Mountain pony, or Section A, is the smallest at up to 12 hh. The Welsh pony, or Section B, can be up to 13.2 hh. The Welsh pony of cob type, or Section C, can do any job – he makes a lovely riding pony and was used to haul slate from the North Wales' mines. The Welsh Cob, or Section D, is usually about 14.2 – 15 hh and is at home in harness and under saddle; he often has a spectacular trot.

Connemara

Welsh Cob (Section D)

Welsh Pony (Section B)

Welsh Pony of Cob type (Section C)

Welsh Mountain Pony (Section A)

Dartmoors are popular riding ponies.

Exmoor

Dartmoor

The Connemara pony originates from Ireland. He is usually sure-footed and an excellent jumper, making him a good competition pony. He can be any colour except piebald or skewbald, and is often grey.

All the British breeds (called native ponies because they originated here) grow thick winter coats, essential for their survival on Dartmoor and Exmoor or in the Welsh hills. You can often guess how a pony is bred by looking at him, because each breed has strong characteristics. Sometimes native ponies are crossed with Thoroughbred horses to try to produce small horses with the qualities of both parents.

Different breeds and colours developed according to where ponies lived. Shetland ponies are small and hardy because in their native Shetland Isles they had to survive on little food. They are incredibly strong for their size and were used as pack ponies to carry large loads of peat and seaweed in panniers.

Highland

Shetland

Highland ponies can carry loads of over 16 stone. Their strength, combined with their kind nature, means they too can do a number of jobs. They are often dun with black markings along their backs called dorsal eel stripes.

Shetland

Highland

Dales

Fell

Welsh

Exmoor
Dartmoor
New Forest

Dales

Fell

Dales and Fell ponies are versatile ride and drive animals. They look very much alike, but the Dales is larger and heavier built.

New Forest ponies have a mixed ancestry, which includes Thoroughbred, Dales, Fell, Dartmoor and Welsh. They are usually easy to handle and comfortable to ride. In the New Forest you will see ponies seemingly roaming free, but all have owners and there are regular round-ups and sales.

New Forest Pony

Horses and ponies are measured in hands and inches, measured from the withers to the ground. A hand is four inches; thirteen hands two inches is usually written as 13.2 hh, and so on. Ponies go up to 14.2 hh and horses are 14.2 hh and over.

Dartmoor and Exmoor ponies are both moorland breeds, but it is easy to tell the difference. Exmoors have 'mealy' muzzles that look as if they have been dipped in a bucket of bran and 'toad' eyes that are hooded for protection against bad weather. The Dartmoor nearly became extinct after the Second World War, but fortunately the breed was saved.

There are exceptions to the measurement rules. Shetland ponies are measured in inches, not hands, and an Arab is always called a horse whatever his size. You will also see show classes for 15 hh hunter ponies, but strictly speaking they are small horses.

Ponies of the World

British ponies have been exported and are now bred all over the world. Their beauty and hardiness has made them as popular for children in other countries as they are here, and sometimes they have even been used to help create new breeds such as the Pony of the Americas.

There are, however, many other pony breeds throughout the world, some of which are now being imported into, and bred in, Britain. Haflingers and Fjord ponies, for instance, are becoming popular and even have their own classes at some shows.

Wherever a pony originated, he will have been bred for a purpose. Breed societies, who register ponies and keep records of their pedigrees, are careful to preserve these characteristics.

The Morgan is an American breed whose height usually varies between 14 hh and 15.2 hh — but a Morgan is always known as a horse, even if he is 14.2 hh or under. He is an elegant but powerful horse who gives a comfortable ride.

The Icelandic horse is always called a horse even though he is no bigger than 13.2 hh. He is most famous for his special gait, the tølt — a running walk which covers the ground at speed but is very comfortable for the rider.

The Pinto can be any height, and is only classified as a breed in America. It may look like a piebald or skewbald, but there are two special colourings — Overo and Tobiano. Both types can have a base coat of white or coloured hairs, but the Overo has 'splashy' markings and the Tobiano has more solid patches of white and coloured hairs.

The Falabella is a breed developed by the Falabella family of Argentina. He is never more than 30 in high — and though he is descended from the Shetland, he does not have his strength and hardiness.

The American Shetland is descended from our Shetland pony but does not look anything like him. He has a mixutre of Shetland, Hackney, Arab and Thoroughbred blood and is used mainly as a harness pony.

The Pony of the Americas is a breed that goes back less than 40 years and began with the crossing of a Shetland stallion and an Appaloosa mare. He is always spotted, stands between 11.2 hh and 13 hh and looks like a miniature horse.

Przewalski's Horse is the last remaining true wild horse, and you can see herds in some zoo parks in Britain. There are now wild herds running in the breed's native Mongolia again. Przewalski's Horses stand about 14.2 hh and have erect manes plus dorsal stripes.

Haflinger

Fjord

Bashkir

The Bashkir is a Russian breed and stands around 14 hh. He has a thick, curly winter coat to help him withstand icy winters. This useful hair is sometimes spun and then woven into cloth!

The Fjord pony looks a little like the wild horses you can see in some zoos. He is always dun and often has zebra markings on his legs. His mane is usually cut so that it stands upright.

The Haflinger is a pretty but powerful pony who comes from Austria. He is always chestnut or palomino and is sure-footed with a long stride.

The Arab can be any size from about 14 hh to 15.2 hh, but is always referred to as a horse. This is often said to be the most beautiful breed in the world, and has had a great influence on many others. Arabs have incredible stamina, which makes them especially good for endurance riding.

Arab

Caspian

Bashkir

Przewalskii

Camargue

The Ariègeois comes from the French-Spanish border. A farm pony, he has hard feet that do not need shoes.

The famous white horse of the Camargue' is really a pony: his height is usually between 13 hh and 14 hh. He is used by cowboys in the south of France to herd the black bulls.

Ariègeois

Australian Pony

& Australian Pony

The Caspian pony looks like a miniature Anglo-Arab. He can be anything between 10 hh and 12 hh, and his kind, willing nature makes him a perfect child's pony. Although he is finely built, he has tough feet that never need to be shod.

The Australian pony has Welsh Section A and B ponies amongst his ancestors. He has been bred as an all-round riding pony and can stand between 12 hh and 14 hh.

Colours and Markings

When you describe a pony, you often do so by his colour and markings. There are lots of different beliefs and sayings about colours – some people think that chestnuts tend to be hot tempered, or that pale-coloured animals are not as strong and healthy as those with rich, dark coats. These stories are probably old wives' tales. You may well prefer one colour to another, but it is unfair to assume that a pony will behave in a certain way because of the colour of his coat. The only thing you can say is that pale coats, such as greys or palominos, show stains more than bays or chestnuts and you will have to spend more time keeping them clean.

There are some confusing rules about colour. For instance, officially there is no such thing as a white horse; they are all grey, even the famous Lipizzaner horses from the Spanish riding school in Vienna, that are sometimes called the 'dancing white horses'. A 'black' horse is rarely black. If you can find a single brown hair anywhere on his body, he is dark brown. Some colours have variations. A dark chestnut is known as a liver chestnut, and a bay may be described as dark or bright bay. Appaloosas (spotted horses) are given different names according to their coat pattern.

The markings on a horse's legs and face all help to make him an individual, and have their own names. Look for whorls, too – areas where the hair grows in a circular pattern.

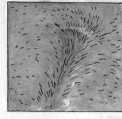

You may occasionally see what looks like a dent on the neck or shoulder; this is called the Prophet's thumbmark and is said to be the sign of a favoured horse.

Alb...

Brown

Stripe

Liver Chestnut

Ermine Spots

Skewbald

Black

Fleabitten Grey

The Suffolk Punch, a breed of heavy horse that originated in East Anglia, is always chestnut – his colour can range from very pale to a dark liver shade, but is usually a strong red chestnut.

Suffolk Punch

Lipizzaner

The Lipizzaners of the Spanish Riding School are always born black or brown. They nearly always turn grey as they get older, though occasionally one will stay bay.

There are several types of face markings, such as the stripe (a narrow white mark down the centre) and the blaze (in the same place, but broader). A star is a white patch between the eyes and can be any shape, and snips are white flashes in the nostril area.

Legs can have white socks or stockings — a sock goes up to the fetlock and a stocking goes up to the knee. Ermine markings are black markings round the coronet. Some breeds, like the Fjord, have zebra markings (horizontal stripes) on their legs.

Appaloosas have five basic coat patterns which are: leopard, blanket, snowflake, frost and marble. The best known one is the leopard pattern with clear coloured spots on a mainly white background, and the least common pattern is the snowflake with white flakes or spots on a dark base coat.

Blue Roan

Strawberry Roan

Pinto

Dun

Piebald

Snip

Chestnut

Bright Bay

Blaze

White Stocking

Cream

Star

Appaloosas

Leopard Spot

ino

Dapple Grey

Blanket Spot

Dark Bay

White Sock

Palomino is a colour, not a breed, and can occur in most types of horse and pony — though you will never find palomino Thoroughbreds or pure-bred Arabs. The ideal coat shade is the colour of a newly minted gold coin, though it can be up to three shades darker or lighter.

Handling Ponies

Even quiet ponies are sensitive and hate loud noises or sudden movements. Remember this when you ride or help to look after a pony and you will find it much easier to make friends with him. Horses have much more sensitive hearing than people, because they have large ears that can be turned to hear sounds from all directions. They cannot see directly behind them or immediately in front, so always approach a pony from the side so he knows you are there. When you go up to him, speak to him before you touch him. This again means that you will not take him by surprise. A startled pony will try to run away and/or lash out with his hind legs. Ponies, like people, must learn good manners. That means he must let you catch him, lead him, tie him up and pick his feet up. If a pony misbehaves when you try to do this, ask your instructor or another knowledgeable adult to help you. Even the smallest pony will be stronger than a big man, so he must learn certain things as a matter of habit. Do not forget to use your voice to praise, scold or command him; for instance, if you nudge his side with your hand and say 'Over' he will soon learn to move over from your voice command alone.

When you turn a pony while he is being led, push him away from you rather than pull him towards you. This gives you more control and means there is less risk of him standing on your foot.

Turning

Quick release Knot

Tied up

Teach him to move off when you give the command 'Walk on' and to halt when you say 'Stand' or 'Whoa'. He should walk out without pulling and you should not have to pull him! If he will not walk out, carry a schooling whip and tap him in the girth area when you give the command. Always look ahead, never back at the pony.

Leading a headstrong pony

Picking up a forefoot

To pick up a forefoot, stand at the pony's shoulder, facing his tail. Run your hand from the shoulder down the back of his leg to the fetlock. Lean against his shoulder and pull the fetlock up; train the pony to lift his foot to a command, like 'Up'. Hold the hoof at the toe, so the pony has to balance himself and cannot try to lean on you.

When catching a pony make sure the field gate is closed behind you and approach the pony from the side. Have his headcollar and a titbit ready, but do not take a bucket of food if there are other ponies about. They may chase and fight each other to get the food and you could get kicked.

Approaching from the left side, offer the titbit in the left hand and slip the headcollar rope round his neck with the right. Quietly slide the headcollar over his nose and put the top strap behind his ears, being careful not to flick or pinch him, and fasten the strap.

Catching a pony

Your headcollar rope should be clipped on with the clip-opening facing backwards to make sure that there is no risk of it digging in to the pony.

When the headcollar is fastened, have a quick look round the pony to make sure there are no obvious cuts or other injuries. Keep hold of the rope in case he decides to walk off.

Strong ponies should be led wearing bridles, which will give you much more control. *Never* wrap the reins or lead rope round your hands – the quietest pony may take fright and can easily break your finger. Always use a bridle when leading a pony on the road.

When turning your pony out, stand facing the gate, unclip the rope (or unfasten the headcollar if you do not leave it on) and stand back quietly. Never slap him on the quarters or chase him off – he may not be so easy to catch next time.'

When you tie up your pony, always use a quick release slipknot like the one shown here.

Turning out

Picking up a hind foot

To pick up a hind foot, stand at his hip, facing his tail. Run your hand from the quarters down the back of the leg to the hock, then take the hand round to the inside of the leg and down to the fetlock; give the command and pull up as before, leaning against his thigh to ask him to shift his balance off that leg. Hold the foot at the toe and keep your arm in front of the leg so he will not pull you backwards and perhaps hurt you if he kicks. Never pull a pony's hind leg out to the side because you could hurt his hip joint. If a pony does not like having his feet picked up or tries to kick you, ask an expert for help. Farriers are the best people, because they know the right techniques and are used to dealing with difficult ponies.

Learning to Ride

Learning to ride is a lot of fun, but you must learn in the right way from an experienced teacher. If a friend offers to teach you on her pony, wait until you have had some proper lessons at a good riding school so that you know the basics. Then you can practise what you learn on your friend's pony and neither of you will get confused!

If you do not know of a suitable riding school, look in a book called *Where To Ride*, published each year by the British Horse Society. It gives information about schools which are approved by the society and are members of the Association of British Riding Schools. There are some good schools that do not belong to these organisations, but if you choose one that does you know that it should have good standards of teaching and horse care.

Once you have found some possible schools, ask if you can go and look round. Weekends will be their busiest time, so do not be put off if they ask you to make an appointment; if you turn up unexpectedly there may not be anyone free to show you round.

The school will probably be busy, but it should look well-run and reasonably tidy, and have a calm atmosphere. There should not be lots of people running about or pitchforks and wheelbarrows left lying around.

If you like the school, check the price of lessons and when they are held. It is always best to have some private lessons first; later you can join a class. Ask if it is possible to meet the person who will teach you — they should be friendly and encouraging.

The school will advise you what clothes to wear for first lessons.

Silk over Skull cap

Riding Hat **Skull cap**

You should never get on a pony unless you are wearing a British Standards Institution approved hat or skull cap with the correct harness. Hats have flexible peaks and are covered in velvet. They should meet BSI 6473 standard (though some also meet the 4472 skull cap standard) and are suitable for all general riding. Skull caps should meet BSI 4472 standard and are usually worn with brightly coloured covers called silks. They are designed for riding at speed, and are worn by jockeys and cross-country riders. The Pony Club says it prefers its members to always wear skull caps when mounted. Some riding schools offer to lend you a hat or skull cap to start with, but it is best to buy your own to ensure a really good fit.

ridi
winter, and
cotton one

Cross~country course

Indoor School

Good grazing

It is important that the school has good facilities. An enclosed outdoor all-weather school (called a manège) is essential and some also have indoor schools. Eventually you will learn to jump. Early lessons will take place in the manège or indoor school, but you might be lucky enough to find somewhere with its own cross-country course. This will have easy, small fences for beginners and larger, more difficult ones for experienced riders. All riding schools should have some grazing land. It should be well looked after, with good fencing (see First Pony).

Safe footwear is essential. Proper riding boots are ideal — choose leather jodhpur boots or high rubber boots. Jodhpur boots are more expensive, because they are made from leather, but they have blocked-in toes that give your foot some protection if a pony stands on it. If you do not want to buy boots straight away, wear shoes with flat soles and a small heel, but no buckles.

Never wear ordinary trainers because your foot could slip through the stirrup, and if you fell off when this happened, you could be dragged. You should not wear boots with heavily ridged soles (which some wellingtons and stable fashion boots have) as these can also get stuck in the stirrups. You can now buy 'riding trainers' designed to look smart and be safe for riding, but do not confuse these with ordinary ones. Buy your hat and boots from a good saddler's shop. The assistants will make sure the hat fits properly and that the boots are safe and comfortable. Never buy a secondhand riding hat — it could have been damaged if a previous owner had a fall.

Jodhpurs are comfortable, but not essential at first. Jeans are adequate as long as they are not too tight, but the seams can rub and pinch. Try jogging trousers or tracksuit bottoms instead. If you are still growing, look on riding school notice boards to see if anyone is selling outgrown jodhpurs in good condition that will fit you; you could save a lot of money.

Riding is hard work! You will be most comfortable if you wear natural fibres like cotton; nylon jackets and anoraks are often sweaty and uncomfortable. Waistcoats and body warmers keep you warm without restricting your arm movement, which is important. If you are riding in the rain, a waterproof
t will protect you and be smart enough for everyday wear. Gloves are essential in
eople like to wear lightweight ones in summer, too. Look for inexpensive wool or
bber pimples on the palm to give a better grip.

First Lessons

Your first few lessons at your new riding school should be private ones with the same instructor. This way you can get to know her and do not have to worry about keeping up with other riders in a group lesson. Even though you are looking forward to learning to ride, you might be a bit nervous. This is quite usual and nothing to worry about — most people are slightly nervous when trying something new.

The pony or ponies you ride on your first lessons will have been specially chosen. They will be the right size for you and will be quiet; they will not get worried if you do something wrong or lose your balance. Even so, remember to approach your pony quietly and in the right way (look back at Handling Ponies to remind yourself).

Your teacher will already have checked that the pony's tack (saddle and bridle) are fitted correctly so that he is comfortable and you can ride him safely. As you learn more about riding you should be able to check this yourself. It is especially important to make sure that the girth, which holds the saddle in place, is tight enough to stop it slipping.

Now you are ready to learn how to mount and dismount, in other words, how to get on and off. For normal riding, you always mount and dismount on the pony's left (which is called the 'near' side). It will be a good idea to practise, later on, mounting and dismounting on the right (which is called the 'off' side) in case this is ever necessary.

Tightening the girth

Small riders with big horses, or anyone who finds mounting difficult, may like to use a mounting block. By using a mounting block you are less likely to pull the saddle to one side as you mount.

Mounting block

Stirrups 'run up'

Stirrups pulled down

Sometimes you may be offered a 'leg-up'. Jockeys mount this way, because they use special light saddles and extra short stirrups that make mounting from the ground impossible. Stand facing the pony's near side, with your left leg bent at the knee. As the person helping you lifts, spring off your right foot and swing it over the saddle as before.

Getting a leg-up

Make sure that the girth is tight enough and the stirrup irons have been pulled down the leathers on both sides. Your instructor will have adjusted them so they should be about the right length for you. Shorten the reins enough to stop the pony walking off and hold them in your left hand. (Some ponies try to nip you when you get on, usually because inconsiderate riders have poked them in the belly with their toes when they mount. In this case, your instructor might tell you to keep the right rein a little shorter than the left one so the pony cannot turn his head to bite you.) You can either hold a lock of the pony's mane, or spread your fingers across his neck so that you can press down and balance on them.

Right   Wrong

Take hold of the stirrup iron by the edge furthest away from you and turn it towards you. This puts the stirrup leather in the correct position so it will not pinch your leg when you are mounted.

Stand facing the pony's hindquarters and put your left foot in the stirrup. If you stand this way and he tries to walk off, the movement will push you up and towards the saddle. If you try and mount facing his head and he walks off, you will be left hopping!

Getting off is easier! Take both feet out of the stirrups, hold both reins in your left hand and rest this hand on your pony's neck. Rest your right hand on the front of the saddle.

Swing your right leg back and over the pony's quarters and land on both feet:

Swivel on your right foot so you are standing straight-on to the horse. Try and keep your toe down so you do not kick him. Balance on your left hand and rest the right one across the saddle.

Push off from your right foot so that your weight is taken on the left one in the stirrup. Swing your right leg over the saddle, being careful not to kick the pony's quarters with your toe, and sit down as gently as you can in the saddle. Try not to pull yourself up with your right hand, or you will pull the saddle to one side.

As quickly and quietly as you can, slip your right foot into the stirrup iron and hold the reins in both hands, just tight enough to stop the pony moving off. Do not push your feet right home in the stirrups — they should rest under the broadest part of your foot.

Riding is all about communicating with your pony. You have to tell him that you want to start, stop, speed up or slow down through a system of signals. This system is called 'the aids' and when ponies are broken in and schooled they learn that different aids mean different things. At first the aids will be very simple. Later on, as you become a better rider and ride more highly trained ponies, you can build up a more detailed system. Learning to ride is like learning to speak a foreign language; you have to learn the basics before you can hold a conversation. To make it easier for you to give the aids and for the pony to understand them, you learn to sit in what is often called a 'good position'. A good position is not just someone's idea of what looks nice. It means you can ride effectively and safely and stay in balance with your pony. At first it may seem difficult to achieve it, but as you get more practice you will find it starts to come naturally. You will find that there is a lot to take in during your early lessons, so your instructor will put your pony on the lunge or lead rein. This means you do not have to worry about controlling the pony and can concentrate on your position. Sit in the deepest part of the saddle, and try to sit up straight without being tense. Your legs should rest against the pony's side without gripping, and your weight should sink down into your heels. Keep your feet level or drop the heels slightly down, whichever is more comfortable. Never let the heels come up higher than the toes.

Hold the reins so that you can feel the bit in the pony's mouth, but do not pull on the reins. They should run between your little and third finger, through your hand and out between your thumb and first finger, with your thumb on top.

Your elbows should be bent and held close to your sides, with your hands just above the pony's withers. Ideally there should be one straight line from your elbow through to the bit, and another running down through your ear, elbow, hip and heel.

The first gait you ride at is the walk, which is slow and comfortable. It may feel as if there is a slight rolling motion at first, but you will soon get used to it. This is because of the way the pony's legs move — watch and you will see that they come to the ground in the order of near hind, near fore, off hind, off fore.

near hind   near fore

To ask the pony to walk on, close your legs round his side and squeeze. With lazy ponies you may have to give a little kick, but always try the lightest aid first. If it does not work, stop and repeat it more strongly. As he walks on, stop squeezing with your legs, keep a light contact with his mouth and let your body absorb the movement of his back. Ready to stop? Sit up straight, close your legs on the pony's sides, and, at the same time, close your fingers round the reins (as if they were two sponges and you wanted to squeeze out the water). As soon as he stops, stop squeezing − if you ask him to continue doing something when he has already done it, you will confuse him.

Lunge lessons are valuable for all riders, even the most experienced ones, because they enable them to put right faults in their position that may affect the way the horse goes.

You need to steer as well as stop and start. To go to the left, look in that direction and 'feel' the left rein with your fingers, (i.e. take up a light contact on the pony's mouth with the left rein). To go to the right, look right and 'feel' the right rein.

You will be able to count 1, 2, 3, 4, to your pony's hoofbeats in walk.

On the lunge

Turning to the right

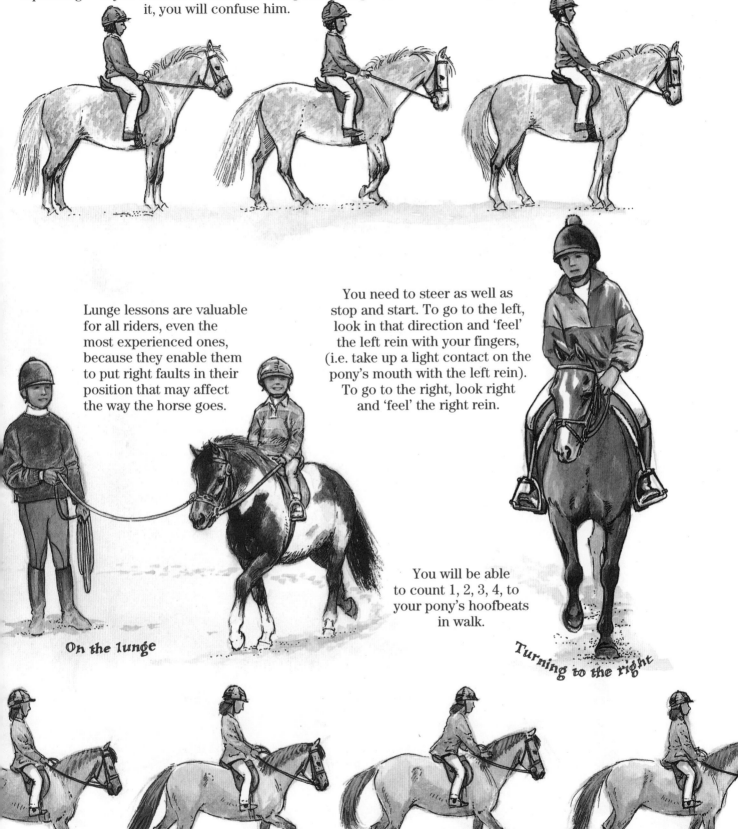

ɟ hind

off fore

Trotting

When you are used to the feel of your pony at walk, you can try trotting. This is the gait that many beginners find most difficult, but it is a bit like riding a bicycle — once you have mastered it, you never forget! A trotting pony feels very different from one who is walking. This is because his legs move in a different way in what are called diagonal pairs: the near fore and off hind move together, and the off fore and near hind. The trot is much more bouncy than the walk, and usually the most comfortable way to ride it is to do the rising trot (or posting, as it is called in America). Do not worry if you find this difficult and uncomfortable at first; you have to get the rhythm of your rising in time with the rhythm of the pony's stride. Hold the front of the saddle if you feel insecure. You will also learn how to do the sitting trot. This can be easy on ponies with a long, smooth stride but is often almost impossible on bouncy ponies with a high knee action.

To ask him to go from walk into trot, shorten your reins a little and squeeze with your legs. As he starts trotting, stop squeezing and try to let his action push you out of the saddle.

With practice you will be able to feel a 1-2, 1-2 rhythm that will help you rise and sit to the rhythm of his stride — try counting as you ride. You will find it easier if you lean your upper body very slightly forwards as you rise. Try not to rise too high or come down hard in the saddle. Remember that trotting takes practice.

Once you have mastered this you will learn how to rise on different diagonals. When you trot on the right diagonal you sit down as the pony's off fore comes to the ground; on the left diagonal, you sit as his near fore comes to the ground. With practice, you can feel which diagonal you are on without looking down. Changing diagonals makes it easier for the pony to carry your weight.

The trot is faster than the walk but slower than the canter.

Walk   Shorten reins, squeeze legs   lean forward & rise   up

Once you can walk and trot on the lunge or lead rein, your instructor may let you try on your own. You will still be in the enclosed school which makes it easier as you practise stopping, starting and steering.

In sitting trot you need to sit up straighter and absorb the pony's movement through your own body. If you bounce or feel insecure, hold the front of the saddle.

Sitting trot

the right diagonal

Sitting on the left diagonal

on the right rein

on the left rein

Now we can make it even more scientific! When you ride a circle to the left (anti-clockwise) it is called 'being on the left rein' and you should trot on the right diagonal. When you circle right (clockwise) you are on the right rein and should trot on the left diagonal. This helps the pony to keep his balance.

sit

up

Cantering

Cantering is the fastest gait at which you will ride on your lessons, and you will go back on the lunge to start with. Most people find it easier than trotting, because the canter is a smooth gait that you can sit to. If you watch a pony cantering you will be able to count a 1-2-3, 1-2-3 rhythm. You will also see that one front leg takes a longer stride than the other — this is called the leading leg, and it is easier for the pony to keep his balance if he leads with the near fore when he canters a circle or turns to the left, and the off fore when he circles or turns to the right. When you canter in the school you should sit up and absorb the movement as you did with sitting trot. Do not worry if you bounce at first, because you need to get used to the movement. It helps to hold the front of the saddle when you are on the lunge. Once you are confident and can relax, you can hold your hands in the normal position.

Once you are used to cantering on the lunge, your teacher will show you how to canter on your own. The aids are a bit more complicated than for walk and trot, because you have to ask the pony to lead on the correct leg.

This pony is cantering to the left, with his near fore leading.

To canter a left circle, trot down to the corner of the school. Just before you get there, sit to the trot instead of rising. Feel the left rein to bend the pony where you want him to go and ask him to canter out of the corner — put your right leg back behind the girth and keep your left leg on the girth.

To canter right, bend the pony slightly to the right, put your left leg back and keep your right leg on the girth.

off hind

When you canter out in the open, it is often easier and more comfortable for the pony if you lean forwards, take your weight out of the saddle and on to your knees and stirrups.

There are very few places where it is safe to gallop, the fastest gait of all. You cannot sit to the gallop — you must take your weight off the pony's back and on to your knees and stirrups. Your reins must be short enough for you to have plenty of control.

Gallop

Near hind   off fore

Near fore
(Leading leg)

When you can ride happily and confidently at walk, trot and canter off the lunge, you will be ready to go for a ride on the roads and bridlepaths. This sort of ride is called a hack. It is fun for you and your pony, and he will probably seem more alert and interested in his surroundings than he does in the school. At first you will be part of a group, with an experienced rider to lead you and another bringing up the rear. Later, if you have your own pony, you will be able to hack out with a friend or on your own. Riding on even the quietest roads means you will meet traffic, so it is important to ride as safely and sensibly as you can. Be observant and make sure other road users know what you intend to do, for instance, look behind you before you move off or cross a road to make sure it is safe. Be alert for things that may make your pony shy or spook, such as plastic bags. Most drivers are considerate and will slow down and move out to give a pony plenty of room when they go past. It is important always to say thank you; a big smile and a nod show the driver that you are grateful and are safer than taking one hand off the reins to signal your thanks. When you ride on bridlepaths or if you have permission to hack on farmland, remember the Country Code. If a gate is shut, leave it shut behind you. Do not canter or gallop if it will churn up the land or bridlepath and always keep your pony in walk if you have to ride through a field of sheep or cows. Always ride on the left hand side of the road. Keep as close to the kerb as is safe on wide, straight roads, but watch out for hazards like drains. On narrow roads, especially those with overhanging trees, it is sometimes safer to move nearer the centre of the road so that drivers can see you.

It is a lot easier if you can open gates without dismounting, but you can only do this if the gate is hung properly and you are on a well-schooled pony.

Otherwise it is safer to dismount, but remember to run up your stirrups before you lead the pony through so they cannot get caught up. Horses are not allowed on footpaths, so stick to bridlepaths. Walkers, however, can use bridlepaths as well, so never canter unless you can see for a long way ahead and you will not churn up the ground too much.

When riding in pairs, go side by side when it is safe to do so but drop back to single file when the road is wide enough to allow cars to overtake. Ride in single file when the road is narrow or you are going round a blind bend.

Make use of gateways and passing places when necessary, and remember to smile and thank drivers who slow down.

If you have to ride past something that you think your pony could shy at, turn his head away from it.

Always look before you move out or change direction, and give the correct hand signal. Read the *Highway Code* and the British Horse Society's road safety booklet.

Never turn your pony's head towards spooky hazards. This will mean that his quarters swing out into the middle of the road, which is dangerous if traffic is coming past.

Be seen — be safe! It is easier for drivers to see you if you and your pony wear reflective, fluorescent gear, especially if it is dull or raining. The safest combination is a belt or tabard for you and leg bands for your pony. Never ride on the roads in the dark. If you ever have to lead a pony on the road in the dark, perhaps from his field to his stable, wear your visibility gear and carry a powerful torch. You can also get flashing lights that clip on to a boot or belt.

Jumping

All horses and ponies can be taught to jump, but some are better at it than others. It is important not to bore a pony by jumping too much, or to overface him with fences that are too big for him so that he loses his confidence. The most important thing about jumping is to stay in balance with your pony so that you do not interfere with him as he takes the fence. This means you have to sit in a slightly different way from the position you use for ordinary riding (or riding on the flat, as it is sometimes called). At first you will practise this new position over poles on the ground and small jumps in the school. They will be so small that it may feel as if the pony is simply taking an extra large stride, but this gives you the chance to get everything right. Some riders find jumping exciting, while others are a bit nervous about it. Tell your instructor how you feel, and she will make sure you enjoy your jumping lessons.

You will start by walking and then trotting over a pole on the ground. Practise folding your upper body forward from the waist, stretching your arms and hands forward to give the pony freedom of his head and neck over the 'fence' and letting your weight sink down through your heels.

If there are ponies and horses of different sizes in the same class, your instructor may put trotting poles on a circle in a fan shape. Small, short-striding ponies can trot through the narrow distances and large, long-striding horses can trot through the wider ones. Trotting poles — three or more poles in a row which are ridden at trot — make the pony think about where he is putting his feet. It is important that they are the right distance apart for his stride so that he can establish a rhythm; your instructor will adjust them, but they are usually between 1.1 m (3 ft 6 in) and 1.4 m (4 ft 6 in) apart depending on the size and stride length of the pony or horse.

Trotting poles

Fan-shape

Before you start, shorten your stirrups by two or three holes. This will help your balance

Cross pole

Shorten stirrups for jumping

Your first proper jump will be a small cross pole about 15 cm (6 in) high, which you will trot into. A cross pole encourages a pony to jump the centre of the fence. There may be a pole on the ground in front of it to make it easy for him to adjust his stride. Your first jumps will all be taken at trot rather than canter, though your pony will probably go into canter when he lands after the jump. Jumping from trot gives you more time to adjust your position, because things happen a bit more slowly.

Once you are confident, your instructor will add a second fence, then a third and eventually even a fourth — this is called a grid of fences. The distances between them will be adjusted according to the pony's stride so it is easy for him to take off in the right place each time. Even though you trot into a grid, your pony will take canter strides between each fence. The next step is to canter into a single fence, which will not be any more difficult than the work you have been doing. You need to keep the pony straight, in balance and in a good rhythm — just as you have been doing in trot.

Jumping grid

Occasionally a pony may decide he does not want to jump and either stop dead (refuse) or duck round it (run out).

Refusing

If he runs out, turn him back to face the jump and approach it in a strong but controlled rhythm. Use your legs firmly and make sure your reins are short enough to help keep him straight — but be ready to let him stretch his head and neck as he takes off.

Running out

If the fence can be jumped from a standstill, do not turn him away from it, use your legs strongly and be careful not to catch him in the mouth when he jumps.

A course of jumps tests your partnership with your pony. If you can take several different fences calmly and in balance, you have done well — Jumping solid fences across country demands even more skill and courage from both pony and rider.

First Pony

When you have had regular riding lessons for at least a year and have had some experience in looking after ponies – perhaps through helping at your riding school – you might be lucky enough to have a pony of your own. But before you start looking for a pony you must find somewhere suitable for him to live.

Some people own their own land and can keep a pony at home. Most have to rent a field and stable at a livery yard, which is a place providing accommodation for horses and ponies. Some riding schools also take animals at livery.

Remember that looking after a pony takes up a lot of time, and you have to take things like school and dark winter evenings into account. It is often better to look for a yard where there are people to help, because this way you know that your pony will be fed and checked properly.

He will also have other ponies for company, which is important. Horses are herd animals and it is not fair to keep one on his own; if you do, he may misbehave because he is lonely.

Many ponies can live out at grass for all or most of the year, provided they have shelter from bad weather. But you should also have access to a stable if it is needed, if your pony is ill or injured, for example.

Look for a field that is well drained and will supply adequate food – the grass should be short and cover the ground well. You should allow about one acre per horse; three acres will support three or four ponies if the land is looked after properly. The best kind of fencing is a thick hedge, which also gives protection against wind and rain. Post and rails is the next best kind. Avoid wire fencing if possible, especially barbed wire – a pony can easily get caught up and injured.

Gates should be hung properly so they are easy to open and close. If possible, keep them padlocked to deter thieves.

Field shelter

If there is not enough natural shelter you must provide a field shelter, which is like a three-sided stable with an open front. If several ponies share it, make sure they have plenty of room.

Deadly Nightshade

Acorns

Green bracken

Yew

Ragwort

Laurel

Some plants and trees, such as ragwort, nightshades, acorns, yew, laurel and bracken when it is green, are poisonous to ponies. Poisonous plants must be pulled up by the roots and burned (away from the field). Trees should be fenced off so the pony cannot reach them.

Some ponies are prone to laminitis, a crippling foot condition thought to be caused by too much rich grass. They must have their grazing restricted and may have to be kept in 'starvation paddocks' with hardly any grass during the spring and summer.

Your pony must have clean water all the time. If there is no trough in the field, fill plastic tubs or bucklets and if necessary stand them in old tyres to stop them getting knocked over. In winter, ice must be broken — you may need to do this twice a day.

Laminitis

If your pony is stabled, perhaps at night during winter, leave the top door open all the time, even in bad weather. He needs plenty of fresh air. Any glass windows should be protected by metal grilles and you should check that there are no nails sticking out or any other hazards on which he could hurt himself.

fresh air

Electric fencing

Electric fencing is useful for dividing a field into smaller sections. You need to introduce a pony to it by leading him up to it and letting him touch it with his nose; he will get a small, harmless shock which will teach him to treat the fence with respect.

Feeding and Watering

If you watch a pony in the field you will see that he spends most of his time grazing. This is because his digestive system is designed to cope with small amounts of food at regular intervals, a fact which must be taken into account when working out what and when to feed him.

During spring and summer, grass will provide the pony who lives out with most of the energy he needs. If he is working hard and perhaps stabled some of the time, he may need extra feed, usually in the form of ready-made coarse mix or horse and pony nuts.

Grass loses a lot of its goodness in autumn and winter, so unless your pony is very hardy and is a good doer (which means he stays in good condition on the minimum of food) he will again need extra food. He will certainly need hay in winter, especially when the ground is frozen or covered with snow. Always buy the best hay you can get. It should be clean and not smell mouldy or dusty; do not offer poor quality hay, as it may make the pony cough. Store it on pallets off the ground, in a dry place; a barn is ideal. If you do not have a barn or shed you may have to manage with tarpaulins, but this is not very satisfactory and you may end up having to throw away hay that gets damp and mouldy.

Water is just as important as food. Your pony must always have clean water available, both in his field and his stable.

Hay Net

Make sure haynets are tied high enough. An empty one will hang down, so make sure there is no risk of the pony getting his foot caught, but also ensure that the haynet is not too high allowing seeds to drop into the pony's eyes.

Soaking sugar beet

Balanced Mix

Soaked sugar beet nuts can be mixed with winter feeds. They must always be soaked for 24 hours before feeding – never confuse them with pony nuts and feed them dry as they will swell in the pony's stomach and could make him very ill.

Your pony will appreciate apples or carrots added to his feed in winter. Cut apples into quarters and slice carrots lengthways so that they cannot choke him. The easiest way to make sure your pony has a balanced diet is to feed coarse mix or pony nuts. These have had the necessary vitamins and minerals added by the feed company.

The Golden Rules of Feeding

1. Feed little and often.
2. Feed according to age, height, bodyweight, temperament and work done.
3. Feed at the same time each day. Horses are creatures of habit.
4. Make any changes in diet gradual.
5. Clean, fresh water must be available at all times.
6. Feed by weight as well as by volume. A scoop of one feed will not weigh the same as a scoop of a different kind.
7. Always buy the best quality hay and feed.
8. Always wait for an hour after feeding before you ride.
9. If you stop riding your pony, cut back his feed — if necessary, omit hard feed and just give hay.
10. If you are not sure what or how much to feed, ask someone experienced.

Your pony must always have plenty of water. Keep suitable containers filled; avoid any with sharp edges.

Field trough

Feed should be stored in strong containers with lids to keep mice and rats out. Plastic dustbins are useful for this; keep them clean and do not let old food collect in the bottom where it will go mouldy. Some ponies will eat happily out of mangers which clip on to doors or fences. Others knock them to the ground; if you have a destructive pony, stand his feed and water buckets in old tyres to stop him tipping them over.

Some stables have automatic waterers. If not, use buckets on the floor. Try to put them where they will not get knocked over (stand them in tyres if necessary) and where hay and feed will not fall into them.

Feed bins

Grooming

Grooming is essential to keep your pony clean and comfortable, but how much you do depends on how you keep him. If he spends all or most of his time in the field, grooming should be kept to a minimum, otherwise you will remove too much grease from his coat, which helps to keep him dry.

All you need to do in this case is to brush off dried mud before you ride him and to keep his eyes, dock and (in the case of geldings) sheath, clean. It is especially important to remove mud from areas that your tack will touch, such as his head and round the girth. If left on, it can rub and cause skin problems.

The pony who is stabled at night and perhaps clipped in winter can be groomed more thoroughly. He will always look smarter than the grass-kept pony, who needs a thick coat for protection, but even the pony who lives out can be made to look nice for summer shows (see Looking Smart).

However you keep your pony, you must pick his feet out at least once a day. This enables you to check that his shoes are in good condition and helps prevent foot infections like thrush. Time spent grooming or brushing your pony is never wasted. It should enable you to spot minor injuries, heat, swellings or other problems.

If his mane and tail are caked with dried mud, use a plastic curry comb to get the worst off. Separate the hairs with your fingers and brush through with a body brush. Try not to use a dandy brush or metal mane and tail comb because they may break the hairs − plastic combs are not so bad.

Use a hoofpick in a downwards direction, from heel to toe. Do not use it in an upwards direction; if the pony moves you might drive the end of the hoofpick into the sensitive V-shaped frog.

Use a stiff dandy brush or rubber or plastic curry comb to remove dried mud. Never use a metal curry comb on your pony − this is only for cleaning the body brush − and never try to brush off wet mud. Be gentle around ticklish or sensitive areas like the belly and head; it is sometimes better to get the worst of the mud off with your hands and then use a body brush or special soft dandy brush.

Use sponges, warm water and a little mild, unperfumed soap to gently clean a gelding's dock and sheath. If you have a mare, sponge her teats clean. You will need to do this every few weeks. The easiest way of keeping the eyes clean is to wipe them with dampened cotton wool, using a separate piece for each eye.

This is what you will find in a well-stocked grooming box: hoofpick, dandy brush, body brush, metal curry comb, rubber/plastic curry comb, sponges, cotton wool, fly repellent (for summer). The 'extras' are a water brush for damping the mane and making it lie flat (called laying a mane) a stable rubber for giving a final polish, and hoof oil and brush for special occasions. A rough cactus cloth is useful for removing stains from light-coloured ponies.

Sponges

Hoof Oil

Body Brush

Fly Repellent

Water Brush

Rubber Curry Comb

Hoof pick

Dandy Brush

Cactus Cloth

Clipped ponies are easier to keep clean, but may be more ticklish and sensitive, so avoid stiff-bristled brushes and be firm but gentle when you use the body brush. Keep the pony warm by folding his rug back and grooming the front half, then folding it forwards while you groom behind the saddle area. The best clips for ponies are trace and blanket clips, which help prevent them sweating but leave enough coat on to keep them warm.

A full tail gives a grass-kept pony protection from flies and can be plaited for shows. Pulling a tail is a job for an expert and pulled tails need to be bandaged regularly to keep them neat.

The body brush is used to remove grease from the coat of a stabled pony. Use it in short strokes and clean it frequently on the metal curry comb, tapping the curry comb on the floor to get the grease out. Never cut a pony's mane with scissors to shorten it, or it will look odd and unnatural. Ask someone experienced to help you pull it.

A few hairs at a time are pulled out from underneath until it is the right thickness and length.

Shoeing

Your pony will need regular attention from the farrier if he is to stay sound and work well. Most ponies need to be shod about every six weeks, and even if the shoes are not worn out, the pony's feet will need trimming. If a pony is ridden on the roads he needs shoes to stop his feet getting split and bruised by the hard tarmac. If he spends all his time on soft ground, perhaps because he is retired or being rested, the farrier may decide he does not need shoes, but he will still need to have his feet trimmed every six weeks. Shoeing does not hurt the pony, because the farrier rasps and bangs nails into parts of the foot that have no feeling. Shoeing is a skilled job and it takes four years for a farrier to train and qualify. It is illegal for anyone but a qualified farrier to shoe a horse.

Shoes for the hind feet have two toe clips to help hold them on. Shoes for the forefeet usually have only one. Racehorses wear special lightweight aluminium shoes called racing plates. These are put on just for the race itself and replaced with ordinary shoes for the rest of the time.

There are two forms of shoeing, 'hot' and 'cold'. With hot shoeing, the farrier burns the hot shoe on to the pony's foot before he nails it on to give the best possible fit — again, it does not hurt. With cold shoeing, he prepares the foot, and nails on a ready-made shoe that he knows is the right size. Cold shoeing does not allow for quite the same degree of accuracy. If your pony loses a shoe or one comes loose, call the farrier out as soon as possible and do not ride until he has put things right, if you do, your pony could hurt himself.

As long as they are handled correctly, ponies soon learn that visits from the farrier are nothing to be afraid of. Foals and young horses and ponies usually see their mothers and other horses shod before it is their turn. Youngsters' feet must be rasped and kept in the correct shape, but they do not need shoes until they are broken in and ridden on the roads.

Check your pony's shoes every time you pick out his feet.

The farrier uses special tools. He will use a buffer to loosen nails before taking off the old shoe with pincers. Hoof parers are used to clip away the part of the foot that has grown too long. The farrier will then rasp the foot to make it level and neat. He nails on the new shoe ensuring that the nails go into the right part of the foot, otherwise he might lame the pony. The nail ends are twisted off, and the points (called clenches) are rasped down.

Loose shoes or risen clenches, where the nail ends come up, mean you need to call out the farrier.

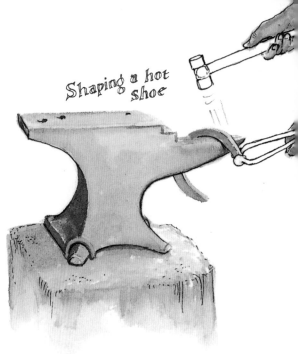
Shaping a hot shoe

Hot shoeing creates a lot of noise, smoke and steam that can look and sound quite alarming, but are harmless to the pony. Your farrier will need somewhere dry, light and clean to shoe your pony if he is to do a good job. He will not appreciate it if the pony is not ready for him, or is wet and muddy!

Fitting studs

If you are competing on hard or slippery ground, you may want to use studs to give your pony a better grip. These screw into special holes in the shoe and come in different shapes for different types of ground.

Paring the foot

Rasping level

Fitting and nailing

Clenches rasped down

Rugs

If your pony grows a thick coat and has a field that provides plenty of shelter, he will be quite happy and warm even i[n]
very cold weather. His coat will stand up and trap a layer of air between it and his skin which helps to keep him warm[.]
If he does not have such good natural protection, or if you want to clip him so that you can work him harder without
him sweating, he will have to wear rugs. He will need a tough outdoor rug — called a New Zealand, because the idea
originated there — to keep him warm and dry outdoors and a lighter weight stable rug if he is kept in at night.

It is best to have two New Zealands, because then you have a
spare if one gets wet or torn. They can be made from many
different materials, ranging from traditional cotton flax to
modern synthetics. The best New Zealands stay in place
very well, but they can slip if a pony rolls a lot and
it is important that you check him regularly, at least
once and preferably twice a day. Stable rugs are
usually made from washable, quilted materials, but
some people prefer traditional jute ones — perhaps
with extra blankets underneath. Whatever sort
you choose, it is important that it is the right
size for your pony and does not rub him. There
are other rugs that can be useful, but these are
the really essential ones.

To find out what size rug your pony needs, measure
from A to B (the centre of the chest to the quarters) and C to D (just in front of the withers to
the top of the tail). Give these measurements to your saddler and tell him what sort of build your
pony has — whether he is fine or cobby, for instance — and he will be able to find you a rug that fits.
If your rug has legstraps at the back, they should be looped one through the other and fastened
to the side they start from, that is left to left and right to right. They are tight enough when
you can fit a hand sideways between the legstrap and the pony;
make sure they are not too tight because they will rub
him, or too loose because then he can catch a
leg in one of the straps if he rolls.

Exercise Sheet

Jute Rug with roller

leg straps

Thatching unde[r] a sweat sheet

Some stable rugs have to be worn with rollers. These need to be
specially shaped so that there is no pressure on the pony's spine.

When you put a rug on, fold it in half (if it is light enough) with the two edges at the front, and the fold at the back, and put it on gently, a little further forward than the place you want it to end up. Unfold the back half and slide the rug back into position so that the pony's coat lies flat. (When you take the rug off, fold the back to the front and lift it off to the side.)

Modern rugs have cross surcingles, but a few people still use old-fashioned ones (usually made from jute) with underblankets and rollers. The underblanket must be folded carefully to stay in place, and rug and blanket secured by a roller. You must make sure that the roller does not press on the spine.

When the rug is in place, do up the front fastening before you fasten any of the others. This ensures that, if the pony is startled, the rug will not slip and get tangled round his legs. When you take it off, do not undo the front fastening until last for the same reason.

Lightweight rugs have a fillet string at the back. This goes under the tail and stops the rug blowing off the pony's back. It should not be tight.

A sweat rug or sheet is useful for drying off a hot or wet pony. It will only work if you put another rug on the top of it to trap a layer of air. You can also put a layer of hay along a wet pony's back and loins and fasten a sweat rug on top; this dries him off quickly and is called 'thatching'.

Rugs are expensive, so look after them! Brush the mud off New Zealands when it is dry and keep leather leg straps clean and supple by saddle soaping and occasionally oiling them.

You will sometimes see clipped horses — especially racehorses — wearing exercise sheets in winter to keep their backs warm.

If your rug has cross surcingles, they are fixed on the off (right) side of the rug, cross underneath the pony and fasten on the near (left) side, at the point where the girth goes. You should be able to fit your flat hand between the surcingle and the pony.

Putting on extra layers

Cotton flax
New Zealand rug

synthetic
stable rug

cross
surcingles

Bridles and Bits

There are many different kinds of bridles and bits, all designed for particular purposes. For instance, well-schooled dressage horses often wear double bridles (which have two bits) but these are not suitable for beginners. Many of the other types are described and illustrated here. There are a number of points which apply to both bridles and saddles (the pony's tack). It is important that a pony's tack is in good condition and fits well. Tack that is in need of repair is dangerous because it could break without warning, and tack that does not fit will make the pony uncomfortable and badly behaved. Imagine how you would feel if you had to wear shoes that were the wrong size! If you have to buy tack, go to a good saddler's shop and ask for advice. Whether you buy new or secondhand, look after it and clean it as often as you can. You should always check a pony's tack before riding him. Is it in good condition? Is it adjusted correctly? Are all the straps in their keepers?

Eggbutt Jointed

Loose Ring

Fulmer

Vulcanite Half moon

French Link

Kimblewick

The most common family of bits is the snaffle, but there are many different types. In general, an eggbutt snaffle stays still in the mouth, a loose ring gives more play and full cheeks help with steering a young or unschooled pony. Illustrated here are some of the ones you are likely to see.

If you need more control with a strong pony, perhaps for jumping, you might be advised to ride him in a pelham or kimblewick. Both can have vulcanite (hardened rubber) or metal mouthpieces. Kimblewicks are used with one rein; pelhams should really have two, but if this is too complicated, pelham roundings will enable you to use just one rein.

When bridling the pony, stand on his nearside and buckle his headcollar round his neck; this gives you some control if he tries to walk off. Put the reins over his head, hold the headpiece in your right hand and let the bit rest in your left.

Pelham

If he does not open his mouth, put your left thumb into the corner of his mouth, where there are no teeth, and press gently. Alternatively, tickle his tongue with your thumb — this works wonders with some awkward customers.

Slip the bit in and slide the headpiece on, guiding his ears through gently. Some ponies dislike having their ears handled, usually because inconsiderate handlers have been rough with them. Adjust the throatlatch (pronounced throatlash) so that the width of your hand fits between it and the pony's face. You should be able to fit a finger between the browband and cavesson noseband and his face.

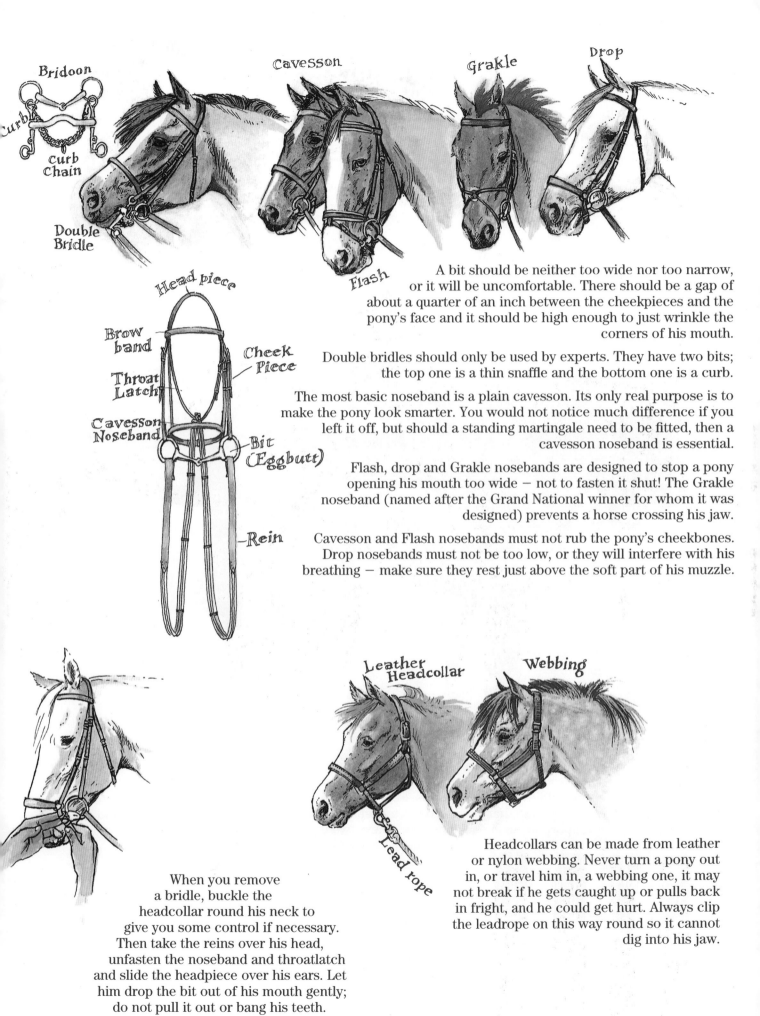

Bridoon

Curb

Curb Chain

Double Bridle

Cavesson

Grakle

Drop

Flash

Head piece

Brow band

Throat Latch

Cheek Piece

Cavesson Noseband

Bit (Eggbutt)

Rein

A bit should be neither too wide nor too narrow, or it will be uncomfortable. There should be a gap of about a quarter of an inch between the cheekpieces and the pony's face and it should be high enough to just wrinkle the corners of his mouth.

Double bridles should only be used by experts. They have two bits; the top one is a thin snaffle and the bottom one is a curb.

The most basic noseband is a plain cavesson. Its only real purpose is to make the pony look smarter. You would not notice much difference if you left it off, but should a standing martingale need to be fitted, then a cavesson noseband is essential.

Flash, drop and Grakle nosebands are designed to stop a pony opening his mouth too wide — not to fasten it shut! The Grakle noseband (named after the Grand National winner for whom it was designed) prevents a horse crossing his jaw.

Cavesson and Flash nosebands must not rub the pony's cheekbones. Drop nosebands must not be too low, or they will interfere with his breathing — make sure they rest just above the soft part of his muzzle.

When you remove a bridle, buckle the headcollar round his neck to give you some control if necessary. Then take the reins over his head, unfasten the noseband and throatlatch and slide the headpiece over his ears. Let him drop the bit out of his mouth gently; do not pull it out or bang his teeth.

Leather Headcollar

Webbing

Lead rope

Headcollars can be made from leather or nylon webbing. Never turn a pony out in, or travel him in, a webbing one, it may not break if he gets caught up or pulls back in fright, and he could get hurt. Always clip the leadrope on this way round so it cannot dig into his jaw.

Saddles

There are many different kinds of saddles, from jumping saddles to those designed for side-saddle riders, and the modern synthetic saddles, but all have one thing in common; they must fit well so that there is no danger of the pony's back or withers being pinched or rubbed. Fitting a saddle is an expert's job best done by a saddler, but, as a rough guide, an adult should be able to get three fingers between the pommel and the withers when the rider is mounted. There should also be a clear channel of daylight along the gullet and the flaps should not restrict the movement of the pony's shoulders.

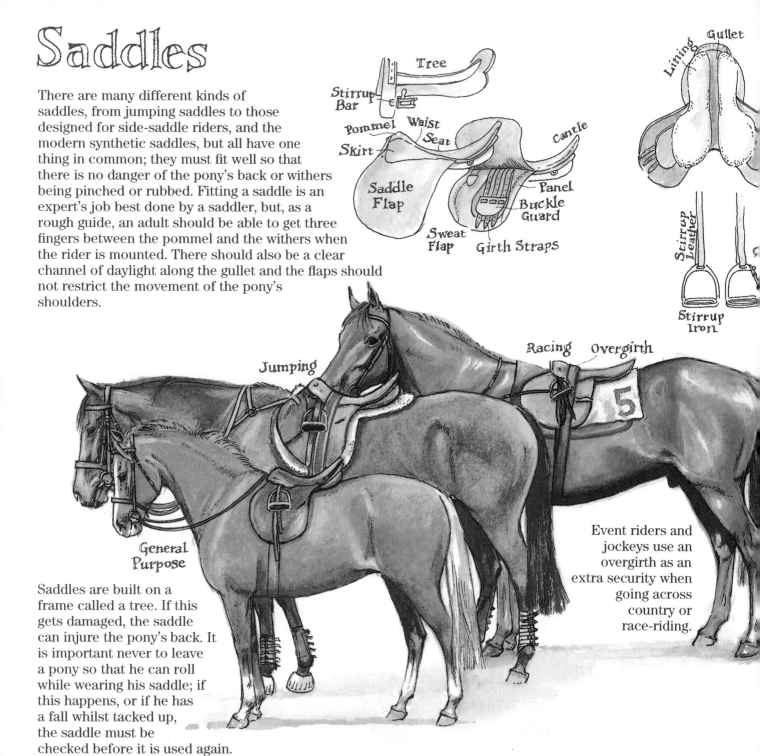

Event riders and jockeys use an overgirth as an extra security when going across country or race-riding.

Saddles are built on a frame called a tree. If this gets damaged, the saddle can injure the pony's back. It is important never to leave a pony so that he can roll while wearing his saddle; if this happens, or if he has a fall whilst tacked up, the saddle must be checked before it is used again.

Most pony saddles are of the general purpose (GP) type. They are designed so that you can do most things in them quite comfortably, from flatwork to jumping, as long as your stirrups are the correct length.

Specialists use different saddles for different jobs. For example, jumping saddles have forward cut flaps and dressage saddles straight flaps so that advanced riders can adopt the safest and most effective positions for the job to be done. General purpose saddles fall between these two types, and racing saddles are very small and light.

A side-saddle has two pommels and a special girth.

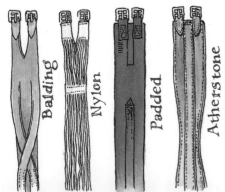

Some ponies are an awkward shape. If a saddle has been fitted as well as possible but still slips back, a breastplate or breastgirth may help. Many racehorses wear breastgirths as a matter of course, and some riders like a breastplate for cross-country riding.

All saddles are kept in place by a girth. This can be made from leather or from washable synthetic materials.

Tack cleaning is important for safety as well as looks. The bit must be rinsed clean every time it is used and the girth kept clean. To clean tack thoroughly, take it apart and wipe the leather clean with a damp cloth or sponge, then apply saddle soap on a sponge that is just slightly damp. Check leather and stitching regularly for signs of wear, and apply a good leather oil or dressing to the flesh (under) side of the leather when your tack needs it.

Stirrup irons must be large enough to allow 1.3 cm (½ in) each side of the widest part of your boot, but not so large that your foot can slip through. Safety irons have rubber rings which pull away from the iron if the rider falls, so the rings must therefore be on the outside.

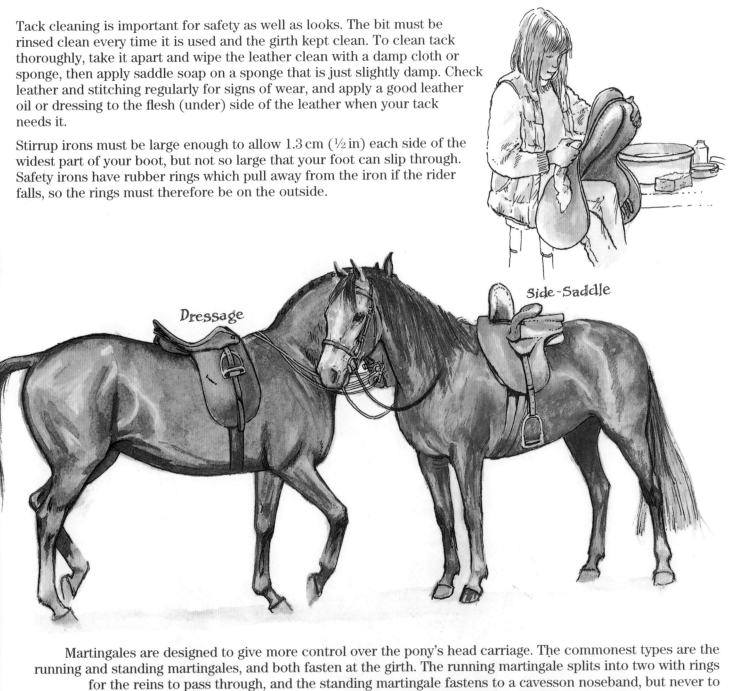

Dressage

Side-Saddle

Running Martingale

Standing Martingale

Numnah

Breast girth

Crupper

Martingales are designed to give more control over the pony's head carriage. The commonest types are the running and standing martingales, and both fasten at the girth. The running martingale splits into two with rings for the reins to pass through, and the standing martingale fastens to a cavesson noseband, but never to any kind of drop noseband or it will restrict the pony's breathing. Numnahs or saddle cloths are often used to keep the underneath of the saddle clean. They must be pulled well up into the gullet to stop them pressing on the pony's spine.

Saddles sometimes slip forwards on little fat ponies with flat withers, so a crupper is used. A crupper is a strap which fastens to the back of the saddle and ends in a padded loop through which the pony's tail goes.

Looking at Ponies

Buying your first pony is both exciting and nerve-racking. It is important to get expert advice before making the final decision, but it is equally important that you are confident that you will enjoy riding and looking after him. Your riding instructor will advise you on how big your pony should be. Obviously you do not want to grow out of him too quickly, but you do not want a pony who is much too big for you either, or you could find it difficult to control him. It is vital that your pony has a nice temperament, in other words, that he or she is friendly and willing. Most people say that geldings are more predictable than mares, but you need to treat each pony as an individual. Some mares can be a bit difficult when they are in season, but this is not always the case. You should not buy a young pony unless you are a very experienced rider and have the facilities and help available to train him. Usually it is best to look for a pony who is at least seven years old, and remember that ponies can work happily well into their teens and even longer. Do not be surprised if your ideal first pony turns out to be older and more experienced than you!

Good looks are not as important as a good temperament, but if a pony's conformation (shape) is fairly correct he will be more comfortable to ride and more likely to stay sound. Ideally his body (excluding his head and neck) should fill a square, so if you drew one round him he would look as if everything were in proportion.
His head should be in proportion to the rest of him and he should have a kind expression. It is nice to see a handsome or pretty head, but it does not matter if he has a Roman nose — you want to have fun with him, not win beauty contests!

Sickle Hocks

Straight Shoulder

His neck should be long enough to give you a feeling of security when you ride him. Ponies with short, thick necks are often strong and ponies with ewe necks (which look as if they have been put on upside down) usually hold their heads too high and are harder to control. A sloping shoulder is preferable to a straight one. A pony with a straight shoulder is often uncomfortable to ride, because he has an 'up and down' action that jars the rider.

His front legs should have flat knees, short cannon bones and pasterns that are not too upright. If you are not sure where all these parts are, check the points of the horse chart.

The quarters and hind legs are the pony's 'engine', and good hocks are very important because they supply the 'thrust' and 'drive'. Cow hocks and sickle hocks are both a sign of weakness.

The perfect pony has not yet been born! All ponies have some conformation faults, and an expert such as a vet will be able to tell you whether they will affect his performance or not.

Poll | Ear | Crest | Mane
Forelock | Forehead | Eye | Cheek Bone
Nostril | Muzzle | Chin Groove | Jugular Groove | Throat | Point of Shoulder

Point of Croup | Croup | Loins | Withers | Back | Point of Buttocks | Tail | Quarters | 2nd thigh

Breast | Elbow | Forearm | Knee | Cannon Bone | Pastern | Heel

Belly | Girth | Back of Knee | Tendons | Fetlock Joint | Coronet

Stifle | Chestnut | Hock | Seat of Curb | Ergot

2 Years
3 Years
4 Years
5 Years
7 Years
10 Years
15 Years
30 Years

Each front and back foot should match its partner, they should be a pair, and should look strong and healthy rather than cracked or crumbling.

Cow Hocks

Experts can tell a pony's age from his teeth. It is possible to 'read' teeth very accurately up to eight years of age, after that it becomes more difficult.

A pony who brushes (knocks one leg against the other) can hurt himself and must wear protective brushing boots. A pony who dishes (throws one or both front legs out to the side) will put extra strain on his limbs. Deviations from straight movement are usually only a problem if they are very pronounced.

Thick Neck

Ewe Neck

Dishing

Brushing

Choosing a Pony

When you are ready to buy your first pony, tell knowledgeable people such as your riding instructor. They often know of ponies for sale that might be suitable, and, while the final decision must be yours, it is important to have expert advice.

You can also look at advertisements in local newspapers and horse magazines. Do not forget to read the advertisements on notice boards in saddler's shops and at riding schools, too.

It is important to ask the right questions when you inquire about a pony for sale. Check his height and age and ask the sellers why he is for sale. There can be many good reasons for this (such as his rider growing too big for him) but you do not want a pony that is for sale because he is too strong or lively for his present owner.

Before you go and see him you should check that he is quiet to handle and ride. He must be good in traffic and easy to catch, shoe and load into a horsebox or trailer. You should not consider a pony that bucks, rears or is said to need a very experienced rider.

When you have found a pony that you would like to buy, ask the sellers if you can bring your instructor or a knowledgeable friend for a second look.

First impressions are important. Does the pony seem calm, and happy to see you? Beware of one who seems nervous or who lays his ears back.

Spend a minute or two talking to the pony and handling him. Will he let you pick his feet up easily or does he object? Is he happy to stand quietly when he is tied up?

Ask to see him standing on level ground. Have a good look at his conformation – does he seem to be reasonably in proportion? Are there any lumps, bumps or scars on his legs that you would need to ask your vet to check?

If possible, see him caught and brought in from the field. This way you can be sure that he is easy to catch and does not mind being taken away from his companions.

If you like what you see, ask to see the pony trotted up in hand; the handler should leave his head and neck free so that you can see his natural movement. He should move reasonably straight without brushing or dishing (see previous page).

A pony that brushes can damage himself. Even if it is only a slight fault, he must wear protective brushing boots. The farrier can help by making special shoes that minimise the risk of injury.

A pony that dishes when he trots may look unsightly but dishing need not be a problem with an ordinary riding pony unless it is very bad.

So far, so good? Then ask to see the pony ridden by his present owner, this way you should be able to check that he is well behaved and is not likely to buck or run away.

Notice what tack is put on him. It should really be a simple snaffle bridle, perhaps with a drop or Flash noseband. Be careful if he wears a stronger bit or tight martingale, this probably means he is not a suitable first pony.

Trying a Pony

Remember that the person who is selling the pony knows him a lot better than you, so do not be worried that you will have to put him through exactly the same tests to get the feel of him. Let his present rider show him off to his best advantage, and watch to see how well behaved and responsive the pony is. Watch how he behaves when he is coming towards, and going away from, home. A pony that naps (hangs towards the gate or stable-yard and is reluctant to go away from it) should be avoided. You should see him ridden on the road so that you can assess how he behaves with traffic, following by car if necessary. Ask the rider to ride him past his own gateway on the way back, if he tries to duck in or is reluctant to go past, this is another sign of napping. If you think you can cope, ask if you can ride him, but if you think the pony is more than you can manage, do not be afraid to say so. A genuine seller will not mind, and will be glad that you have not wasted his time. Take things slowly when you first get on the pony. Check that the girth is tight, that the stirrup leathers are the right length and that he stands obediently. Try to keep your aids light but clear when you move off.

If possible, ride him first in an enclosed school or manège. If one is not available, pick a corner of the field. Walk round until you get the feel of him, then ask for trot and practise changes of direction and gait.

When you feel you are used to him — and only if you feel confident — ask for canter in the corner of the school or field. Again, try some changes of gait and direction.

His current owner should already have ridden him over a few small jumps for you. Now you can try, starting with a small cross pole that can be jumped from trot. Is he happy to jump going away from home as well as towards it? You do not need to jump big fences, even if his present owner did; two feet is high enough to show you how he jumps.

By now you should know whether or not you like riding him. If you do, it is often a good idea to come back the next day and try him again, if possible — especially if someone can take you for a short hack on the road. You should not need to see a pony more than twice to make up your mind.

If you decide to buy him, arrange to have him vetted as soon as possible. The vet will check his eyes, heart and lungs and make sure there are no signs of lameness. It is sensible to insure the pony, at least for payment of veterinary bills, as soon as he is paid for and becomes yours.

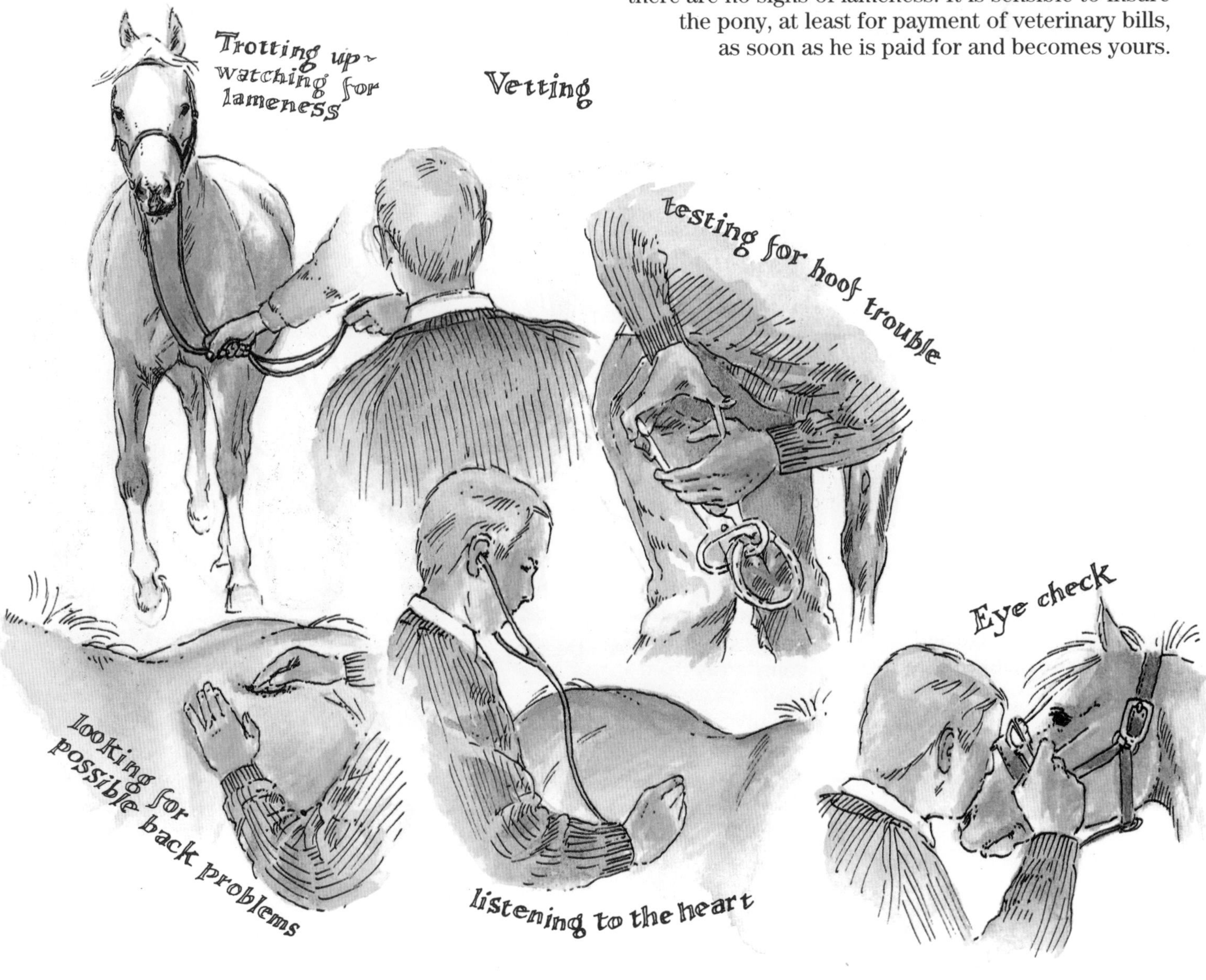

Trotting up ~ watching for lameness

Vetting

testing for hoof trouble

Eye check

looking for possible back problems

listening to the heart

You will be anxious to get your new pony home as soon as possible, but there are a few preparations to make first. It is a good idea to arrange insurance for him straight away — there are lots of companies specialising in horse insurance, so ask your vet which ones he recommends. If the pony is going to be stabled part of the time, get the stable ready for him before he arrives. Put down an extra deep bed, as he will probably roll, and put in a full haynet and plenty of clean, fresh water just before he arrives. Some livery yard owners like even grass-kept ponies to be stabled for their first 24 hours in new surroundings, but others will prefer him to go straight into his new field. His previous owners may offer to deliver him for you, but if this is not possible you will have to arrange your own transport.

If you do not have a trailer or horsebox you will have to hire transport or ask experienced friends to bring him home for you. It is often best to hire a professional transporter who is used to handling horses and is a good driver, because this will ensure that the pony has a comfortable journey.

You will need to protect your pony with travelling gear. Use boots or bandages on his legs in case he knocks himself — boots are easier to put on. Bandages must be applied over padding and you should ask an experienced person to show you how to put them on. You can use separate knee and hock boots or long travelling boots that cover all the vulnerable areas.

Use a leather headcollar, never a nylon one, for travelling. Leather will break if he panics and struggles, but nylon will not give and he could hurt himself. A poll guard gives extra protection to the top of his head in case he throws it up.
Some people like to use a tailguard for extra protection. This fastens over the tail bandage and ties to a surcingle or roller.

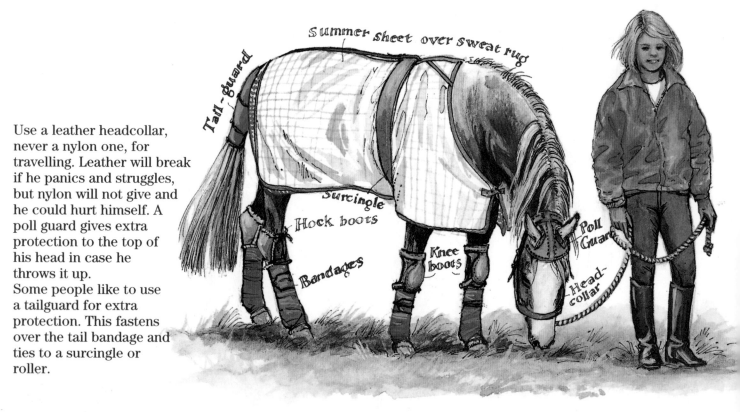

A tail bandage will protect the dock (top of the tail) if he leans back to balance himself. Start bandaging at the top of the tail and leave an overlap; fold this over the first turn and bandage over it. This will help the bandage grip, and you can then wind the bandage down firmly but not too tightly, overlapping half the previous turn each time. When you reach the bottom of the dock — where the bones finish — bandage back up and fasten the tapes, tucking in the loose ends. Bend the tail back into shape gently.

Bandaging a tail

Tail Guard

The pony may need to wear a rug to protect him from draughts, especially in a trailer. It could be a light cotton summer sheet or a warmer rug, depending on the weather. If there is a danger of him sweating, use a sweat rug with a light sheet on top.

Loading

The pony should have a haynet in the box or trailer to keep him occupied on the journey.

Before you load him, check that the vehicle is parked so that the lowered ramp is stable and the interior looks light and inviting. Ask someone experienced and confident to lead him in.
The ramp should be put up quickly and quietly. It is important to stand to the side of the ramp, not directly underneath it, in case it is dropped or the pony kicks back.
Tie him to a piece of string attached to the tethering ring, not directly to the ring. This is another safety precaution — if he panics, the string will break.

Settling Down

When your pony arrives at his new home he
will probably seem a bit excited or worried.
This is quite natural, because he is in strange
surroundings with strange horses and
people, but nothing for you to worry about.
However, you do need to be extra careful
when you handle him, and to make sure you
have someone experienced to help you.

Try to bring him home in daylight so he can
see his new home. If you can pick a time
when the yard is likely to be quiet, so much
the better. The most important thing is to let
him relax, so try and make sure that he has
peace and quiet. Your friends will probably
want to come and see him, but ask them to
wait until he has settled in and is starting to
feel at home.

Some ponies settle down in a new home
straight away, but others take longer. You
should find that by the end of the first week
he is starting to relax. You can help by giving
him a routine, so that he knows when he is
going to be fed and so on.

It is a good idea to put a bridle over the headcollar when you
unload the pony at his new home. This gives you more control.
If he is to be kept in at first, take him to his new stable and
make sure that he has water and a full haynet. Take off his
travelling things and leave him in peace as soon as it is safe to
do so.

When he is turned out for the first
time – or if he has to go out straight
away – it helps if he can go out at first with
just one quiet pony. Do not worry if this is impossible;
there may be some kicking and squealing as the other
ponies get used to the newcomer, but they will soon
settle down.

Remember that
you have to get to
know each other. Spend
time with him, and be quiet
but firm when you handle
him. This way you will
become more confident
with each other.

If the pony is not freeze marked, it is a good idea to have this done to deter thieves. Freeze marking is painless; your pony will probably be marked in the saddle area and will be given an individual number that will enable him to be identified anywhere. On darker ponies, the hairs on the freeze marked area grow back white; on greys, the marked area has bald letters and numbers and needs to be kept clipped to show up.

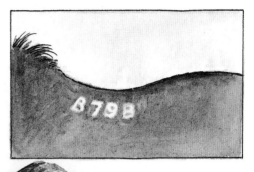

He will soon work out his place in the herd. Some ponies are naturally bossy, while others give way to more dominant characters. Your pony may get a few bites or kicks at first, so check him carefully each time you catch him.

You should also security mark your tack with your postcode. Leather can be marked with ultra violet pens or special stamps, and bit rings and stirrup irons can be engraved with engraving pens. The crime prevention officer at your local police station will give you free advice about security marking.

It is a good idea to leave a leather headcollar (not an unbreakable nylon one) on the pony for the first few days, so that he is easy to catch.

Make sure you have someone with you when you turn him out to help keep the other ponies away from the gate. Turn his head to face the gate, unclip the leadrope and step back. This way there is less danger of you getting kicked if he bucks or gallops off.

A New Pony

You will be anxious to ride your new pony, but it pays to be patient. He will need at least a day out in the field to settle, and you should take things gently at first. Even if he is a very experienced pony, he needs to get used to a new rider. If there is an enclosed schooling area available, it is a good idea to ride here at first. Stick to the basics and get the feel of your new pony; practise turns and transitions and make sure he understands what you are asking him to do. Do not jump him until you have got to know him better and have someone to help you. If you do not have a schooling area, you will have to ride in a corner of the field or on the roads. It is not a good idea to ride where other ponies are turned out, so try to find a time when they are out of the way. Hacking out need not be a problem, especially if you can find a friend on a quiet pony to go with you. Keep your early rides very steady and try to find some quiet routes, even if you know your pony is quiet in traffic. If you have to ride out alone on a new pony, be particularly careful and unadventurous. Do not, for example, jump anything, however small; if you fall and the pony runs off he may not be familiar enough with the area to go home.

Riding on your own is very different from riding on a lesson when you have someone telling you what to do all the time. Decide what you are going to do — when you are going to trot, where you are going to ride a circle or change the rein — well in advance.

No matter how well you get on with your new pony, it is still important to have lessons. This will help you to learn new skills with him and stop you falling into bad habits.

When you hack out, try to go with just one other person on a quiet pony at first. If you go out in a large group, your pony may become excited.

When it is safe to ride two abreast, keep your pony on the inside if he is unsure of his surroundings. If he is quiet and well behaved, take it in turns to go in front so he does not get used to always being in the same place.

All ponies should be capable of being ridden alone as well as in company. When you go out alone for the first time, pick a route you have been round before and make sure someone knows where you are going and when you expect to be back.

As you and your pony get to know each other, you can become more ambitious. You can practise the things you learn on your lessons, but be careful not to bore him by always doing the same thing. He needs a variety of work such as hacking, flatwork and jumping to keep him interested.

Sickness and Health

If you look after your pony well, he should stay happy and healthy most of the time. However, just as you are bound to get colds and small injuries, so may he sometimes be unwell or injure himself.

It is important to know the danger signs so that you can spot when your pony is ill. Normally he should have a healthy coat, bright eyes and be interested in life. If you are in any doubt, call the vet; it is better to be safe than sorry, and in some cases, such as colic, delay can be fatal.

There are regular preventive measures that must be taken to keep your pony healthy. For instance, it is important that he is wormed regularly and that droppings are picked up from the paddock as often as possible to keep the worm count low.

It is also important that he is vaccinated against flu and tetanus.

Watch out for:
1. Your pony becoming listless and apathetic, and perhaps going off his food.
2. The pony sweating and becoming restless.
3. His coat suddenly becoming dull and staring.
4. His droppings changing consistency and becoming either hard or runny.
5. His urine changing colour. Healthy urine is clear to pale yellow and he should not be struggling to stale (pass water).
6. A discharge from the nostrils, swollen glands or a habitual cough.
7. His breathing rate and temperature altering from normal (8−12 breaths per minute at rest, and 38°C).

Ask your vet for a proper worming programme. Wormers come in paste form, which is directed into the corner of the mouth with a syringe, or granules which are mixed with his feed. Some ponies refuse to eat food which has wormer in it even if the taste is disguised with molasses or sugar beet!

worming with a syringe

keeping a mouth open

Taking a temperature

It is important that sharp edges are rasped from the pony's teeth so that he can eat properly and his bit is comfortable. Your vet may use a special gag to keep the pony's mouth open while he does this.

Take a pony's temperature by inserting an ordinary clinical or digital thermometer into his rectum (back passage) − it makes it easier to lift his tail if you put a tail bandage on first. Grease the thermometer with petroleum jelly and wash it in tepid water containing disinfectant afterwards. The reading should not be more than half a degree different either way from 38°C (100.5°F).

To count a pony's breathing rate, stand behind him while he is relaxed and count each rise and fall of the flanks. A sick pony should be stabled and kept warm and quiet. Your vet may want you to put a rug and stable bandages on the pony. Stable bandages are put on over padding from just below the knee or hock to the coronet. If you bandage one foreleg or hind leg, you must bandage the other to ensure both legs are supported.

Your vet may ask you to give the pony a bran mash, which has a laxative effect. Put a scoop of bran in a bucket and pour boiling water on it until all the flakes are wet and a bit sloppy. Add about 28 gm (1 oz) of salt and leave to cool. Sliced apples or carrots may tempt the pony to eat it.

Bran Mash

Putting on bandages

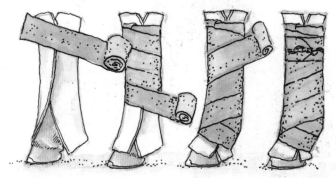

Make sure that bandage tapes or fastenings are rolled to the inside. Wrap Gamgee or similar padding round the leg and start your bandage just below the knee or hock holding the bandage at a slight angle to the leg.

Leave a loose end about 10 cm (4 in) long; make your first turn, then fold the loose end down and bandage over it.

Continue bandaging down, each turn overlapping the previous one by a third to a half of the bandage's width. When you reach the coronet, the shape of the pony's leg will help you turn and bandage up it again.

Aim to finish where you started, and tie the tapes on the inside or outside of the leg. Never tie them at the front, where they will press on bone, or at the back, where they could damage tendons.

First Aid

If you find that your pony is ill or has hurt himself, try not to panic. Some problems can be dealt with quite safely at home, especially if you have someone experienced on hand to help you. Others need the attention of a vet, and the golden rule is that if you are not sure what to do, or the pony is in distress, ring the vet. The commonest problems are lameness, cuts and puncture wounds. You may also have to deal with colic, or find that your pony has contracted a skin infection of some kind. Keep two first-aid kits on hand where your pony is kept (one for horses and one for humans; mark them clearly so they do not get confused!).

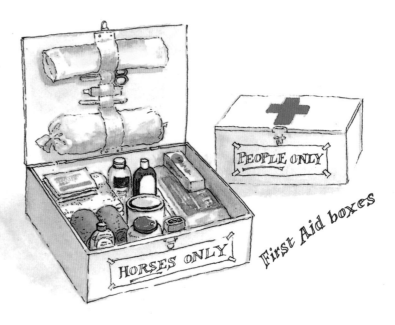

First Aid boxes

The easiest way to spot lameness is at the trot — only very bad lameness shows at the walk. The pony should be trotted up on a long rein, on a firm, level surface. Isolating the lame leg is not always easy, but in foreleg lameness the pony's head will go up when the lame leg hits the ground and nod down when the sound one comes down. The most common site of lameness is the foot.
Your vet will use special hoof pincers to check for painful areas — perhaps caused by bruising.

Hind leg lameness is harder to spot, and you need to watch from behind as the pony is trotted up. You may be able to see the hindquarters on the affected side raised as the lame leg hits the ground, because the pony tries to avoid putting weight on it.

Head going up

Lame leg hitting the ground

Quarters raised jerkily

Lameness in hind leg

Feeling for swelling or heat

Check that there is no obvious cause, such as a stone lodged in the hoof, then run your hand down the pony's leg to detect swelling or heat; feel the other leg to compare the two.

Make up two first-aid boxes, one for horses and one for humans. A basic horse one should contain scissors, a thermometer, cotton wool, Gamgee tissue, bandages, Animalintex poultice, wound dressings and wound powder. Ask your vet what else he recommends.

Some ponies are prone to laminitis, a condition which affects the sensitive structures inside the feet. It is very painful and the pony will often try to take the weight off his front feet. The vet will prescribe drugs to help, and the pony must be kept off rich grass because it is thought that too much rich food is a contributory factor. Laminitic ponies often need to be kept in 'starvation paddocks' in spring and summer.

Laminitis

Colic

Colic is a painful stomach ache that can be mild, severe, or even fatal if the intestines twist. At the first signs — sweating, restlessness, biting or kicking at the flanks, pawing the ground — call your vet, who can prescribe pain relieving drugs and if necessary operate on the pony.

Cold hosing

Swelling and heat at the back of a foreleg cannon bone could mean that the pony has sprained a tendon. Call your vet straight away; you may be advised to hose the leg with cold water or apply an ice pack while waiting for him to arrive.

Injuries and Infections

It is important to check your pony thoroughly at least twice a day to make sure that he has not hurt himself or got caught up. This way you can spot and treat small wounds straight away; if they are unnoticed and left untreated, they can become infected and cause problems. Make sure that your pony's tetanus vaccinations are kept up to date; your vet may want to give him a booster in some cases. Try to keep calm, because wounds often look worse than they are. If the wound is spurting bright red blood, take emergency action and get someone to call the vet immediately, otherwise, you can clean the wound and assess whether or not it needs veterinary attention. Your daily checks will also enable you to spot problems such as mud fever or ringworm as soon as they start. Hygiene is vital for all first aid, and skin problems are no exception. Ringworm, for instance, can be spread from one pony to another — or even to humans — so take suitable precautions.

Control the bleeding

Gamgee under a bandage

Cleaning the wound

When dealing with a wound, first control the bleeding. For small wounds, hold a pad of lint gauze against it (do not use cotton wool, or bits will stick to the injured area). If the blood is spurting, apply a pressure bandage — an elastic or crepe bandage fastened tightly over a Gamgee pad — and call the vet immediately. If the wound obviously does not need stitching, clean the area with lukewarm water containing disinfectant; make sure it is diluted according to the manufacturers' instructions, because if the solution is too strong it may damage the tissues. Be gentle, trickle water on to the wound rather than rubbing at it. If the wound is fresh and you think it may need stitching, do the minimum cleaning with lukewarm water only to stop it becoming contaminated. Do not use disinfectant or apply any ointment or powder, your vet will only need to take it off again. Cover the wound with lint or Gamgee under a bandage until the vet arrives. Puncture wounds can be more serious than they look. If the cause of the injury is still there — perhaps because the pony has trodden on a nail or a thorn is embedded in his flesh — your vet needs to remove it. If a joint or tendon sheath is affected, veterinary help is vital. Puncture wounds need to be kept clean and usually have to be poulticed to draw out infected matter.

Puncture wound

Foot Poultice

Sweet itch is a distressing condition thought to be caused by an allergy to biting midges. The pony will rub his mane and tail bare to try and relieve the itching; he should be stabled during the hours when the midges are at their worst, and your vet will advise you on products that can be applied to the affected areas. Lice also cause irritation. They are quite common in winter and spring, and your vet will recommend insecticidal washes and powders.

Ringworm usually starts round areas where tack touches the skin, such as near the girth or on the face. The hair falls out in small patches and this highly contagious condition can spread to the whole body area. It is spread by contact and humans can catch it. Your vet will prescribe powders to mix in feed and special washes to treat him, his tack, rugs, grooming kit and anything he has been in contact with.

Botflies lay their small, yellow eggs on ponies and horses in late summer, usually on the legs. They should be removed either by brushing with a stiff dandy brush or by scraping with a special bot knife.

Girth galls are often caused by ill-fitting tack — particularly leather girths in bad condition — and bad management. The pony must not be ridden until they have healed. They can be prevented by keeping the coat free from dried sweat and mud in the girth area and ensuring that tack is clean and supple. If your pony has sensitive skin, use a soft padded fabric girth and wash it frequently. Always pull his legs forward after girthing up to ensure the skin is not pinched into folds.

Mud fever and cracked heels occur in cold, wet weather. The heels and sometimes the leg areas become scabby, cracked and sore and in bad cases the pony may be lame. You need to remove the scabs by washing with a special medicated shampoo and apply a soothing ointment such as zinc and castor oil ointment.

Behaviour Problems

As you get to know your pony, you will build up a relationship with him. Hopefully you will enjoy riding and looking after him, but inevitably, there will be times when you come across problems. It is then important to work out whether the pony is frightened, confused or naughty, and to deal with the problem accordingly. Do not try to solve problems alone, always get help from a knowledgeable adult such as your riding instructor. A frightened pony will look tense and worried, as if he wants to run away from whatever is bothering him. He may snort or lay his ears back. A confused pony will not do what you want him to because he does not understand your signals. A naughty pony may try and take advantage of you because you are not firm enough (remember that you can be firm *and* kind).
It is important to stay calm, no matter how annoying the problem, and to sort out small problems before they become big ones!

← give and take ⇒

If your pony breaks away when tied up, clip a lunge line to his headcollar and pass the other end through a tethering ring. When he pulls back and tries to break away the handler can 'give and take' on the line until the pony realises he cannot get away. Always tie ponies to a piece of breakable string attached to a tying-up ring, never directly to the ring; a struggling pony could break his neck.

A pony that is difficult to catch should be turned out in a leather headcollar with a 15 cm (6 in) loop of breakable twine attached to it. Take a shallow bowl of titbits into the field and clip the leadrope quietly to the loop as he eats, rather than grabbing at his head. Always reward a pony for being caught.

If the pony runs off when you try to catch him, do not chase him or try to herd him. Walk away and leave him until he is ready to be caught and have his reward. Do not feed him, and if necessary leave him out all night. He must learn that refusing to be caught is unpleasant because he will not get his feed.

loop of twine

Lead~rope attached to twine

If your pony is difficult to bridle, it is probably because someone has been rough with him and banged his teeth or hurt his ears. It may help to remove the reins and bit and put on the bridle as if it were a headcollar. Fasten the bit on one side, open the pony's mouth by sliding your thumb carefully into the gap at the side of his mouth, gently slip the bit in and, finally, fasten the other side and the reins. With gentle handling you should eventually be able to bridle him as normal.

fastening the bit

Most ponies are good with the farrier, but if yours is not he needs to be shown that this is not an unpleasant experience. Start by picking his feet up frequently and tapping them with a dandy brush; once he is used to this, tap them with a hammer. A patient but firm farrier is the best cure!

loading

Picking up feet

Never lose your temper with a pony that does not want to load into boxes or trailers. A bridle over his headcollar will give you more control, and the vehicle should be parked so that the interior is light and inviting. Two experienced helpers can link hands round his quarters or use lunge lines fastened to the vehicle and crossed over behind him to persuade him to go up the ramp. It is often worth hiring an experienced professional transporter for a morning to help you.

A pony that bites or kicks must be punished immediately. Tell him 'No' sharply and give him one hard smack, preferably with a stick on the girth area. If he takes you by surprise and bites you, a single smack on the nose can be effective. Make sure you have not provoked his bad temper by handling him roughly, for example using a stiff brush on a sensitive area or jerking up the girth. Always treat ponies that are known to kick with caution.

biting

Kicking

Fit girth gently

A pony that kicks or bites when saddled has probably been girthed roughly. Having checked that there are no injuries or sore places, place the saddle gently on his back and slide it back into the correct position so the hairs lie flat. Fasten the girth loosely at first, then tighten it gently, one hole at a time.

Riding Problems

Even the best-behaved pony will buck or shy sometimes, perhaps because something has startled him or because he is feeling well, full of high spirits and wants to let off a little steam. But when something becomes a habit it is a problem, and you need experienced help to solve it.

Many riding difficulties start because the pony does not understand what you are asking him to do. Make sure that your aids are clear and correct. Never lose your temper when you are riding or schooling, because you will only make the situation worse. If you do need to hit a pony, do it once behind the girth. Always check that his tack fits properly and his teeth are not too sharp. If a pony is uncomfortable or in pain because his saddle pinches or his teeth need rasping, he will understandably object to being ridden. You also need to make sure that he is not getting too much to eat, because too much hard food or rich spring grass can often make a pony silly.

Some ponies tug the reins out of their rider's hands so that they can get their heads down to eat. Fitting grass reins can help – these can be made of baler twine (or a similar string) and go from the bit ring to the D-rings on the saddle. They should be short enough to stop the pony getting his head down but not so short that they interfere with his being ridden.

Grass reins

If your pony tries to buck, sit up and slightly back, and take a good hold on the reins to try to prevent him putting his head down. At the same time, use your legs to send him forward and your voice to let him know that he is behaving badly. Habitual buckers should be schooled by an experienced adult.

Nothing is more frightening than a pony who rears. If it happens to you, lean forwards and keep the reins loose when he is in the air, so there is no risk of pulling him over backwards. Rearers are dangerous and only experienced professionals should attempt to reschool them.

Bucking

Rearing

A pony who naps — hangs towards home, refuses to leave the yard or other ponies, or tries to turn round and head for home — should be dealt with by a strong, experienced rider. Techniques include turning him in tight circles until he is disorientated and then riding him forward. Never encourage a pony to nap by riding out and then turning and retracing your steps, always take a different route home.

Pulling

Ponies who refuse to jump may have been asked to jump too often or too high. They may also have been jabbed in the mouth by a bad rider.

If your pony has been over-jumped or over-faced, do something different for a few weeks then go back to basics; start with trotting poles and then introduce a small cross pole. Check your riding and do not jump more than twice a week.

A pony who pulls is often excitable or frightened of the bit because he has been ridden roughly. He needs schooling to reinforce obedience, and your instructor may recommend a change of bit or noseband. Most ponies are stronger in company than alone, and some need a different bit (such as a pelham) for jumping, especially across country.

Shying

Laziness

Most ponies will shy away from things that frighten them, which can range from plastic bags blowing about to birds flying out of the hedge. They will sometimes also shy at unfamiliar things in familiar places. If you think your pony will shy at something, try to stay relaxed. Turn his head away from the spooky object and use your legs to drive him past it. Never hit a pony for shying, or you will punish him for being frightened and make things worse. A lazy pony who refuses to answer the leg must be re-educated. If he does not answer the aid, tap him once with a schooling whip; if he still does not answer, give him a harder tap. Do not just keep kicking; he must learn that it is much more pleasant to obey a normal leg aid.

Enjoying your Pony

There are all sorts of activities that you and your pony can enjoy together, from local shows to sponsored rides. It is a good idea to join your local Pony Club branch or riding club, because they will organise shows and outings. Go and watch a few shows and other events. You will be able to work out what sort of classes will suit your pony – remember that looks are not everything, and the 'ordinary pony' who is well schooled can compete successfully in everything from dressage to cross-country events. Do not be too ambitious at first. Look for classes that are aimed at the novice rider and pony, or that will bring out his and your particular talents. For instance, an obedient, sensible pony might do well in family pony classes.

Gymkhana games demand an agile pony and rider. It takes confidence and lots of practice to do well.

Family pony classes are designed for ponies who can be ridden by most members of the family. They usually involve specially built hazards for pony and rider to negotiate, such as opening gates and walking past flapping plastic sacks.

Gymkhana Games

Sponsored rides, which often have optional jumps, usually start at about ten miles and are organised to raise money for charity. Your pony needs to be reasonably fit to take part.

Showing

Dressage

Showing classes are judged on the pony's conformation and schooling. Both you and he will need to be immaculately turned out. The judge will often ask you to give an individual show – walk, trot and canter on each rein for example – for which he must be well schooled and beautifully behaved.

Dressage competitions give you the chance to show how well schooled and obedient your pony is. Each test consists of a series of movements in walk, trot and canter and you will also be marked on your riding ability.

Show Jumping

Novice show jumping competitions for ponies are over a course of eight to 12 fences at a height of about 61 cm (2 ft). There are four faults for each jump knocked down, three faults for the first refusal, six for the second, and three refusals means elimination. Everyone who goes clear in the first round goes through to a jump-off, usually against the clock, when the winner is the pony with the fastest clear round.

Hunter Trials

Hunter trials are usually run over courses of about one and a half miles, so your pony needs to be fit. Fences will be natural ones such as logs and you will probably have to cope with hazards such as ditches and water.

There are thousands of local shows held each spring and summer. They have classes to suit everyone, from show jumping to fancy dress competitions.

Condition and turnout classes are a good introduction to shows. You will be judged on how clean, tidy and well turned out you and your pony are, and the judge will take into account whether he is stabled or lives out.

'Condition & Turnout'

Looking Smart

For special occasions, you will want to make your pony and yourself look as smart and correct as possible. This can involve a lot of work, but need not be expensive — for instance, you can often buy good secondhand riding clothes quite reasonably. If your pony lives out all or most of the time it is unfair to do anything that would lessen his natural protection. While it would be best not to trim off his whiskers or pull his tail, you can give him a bath in warm weather and plait his mane and the top of his tail for shows. Stabled show ponies usually have their muzzles and ears trimmed and their manes and tails pulled. Native ponies and Arabs are shown with full manes and tails and should not be plaited, but they must be clean and tidy.

a trimmed tail

You can tidy, thin and shorten his mane by pulling it. Use a mane comb and start with the longest hairs from underneath, pulling only a few hairs at a time. Pull manes and tails over several days, preferably when the pony is warm from exercise and the pores are open so that the hairs come out easily. Never cut a mane with scissors — this leaves blunt ends and makes it look unnaturally thick.

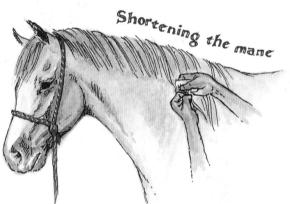

Shortening the mane

To plait a mane, dampen with water or hair gel and divide into sections. Plait each section and fasten the ends, preferably with a big, blunt needle and thread, though some people use rubber bands. Roll up the plait and fasten with a couple of stitches or by looping the band round. There should always be an odd number of plaits down the neck plus one for the forelock.

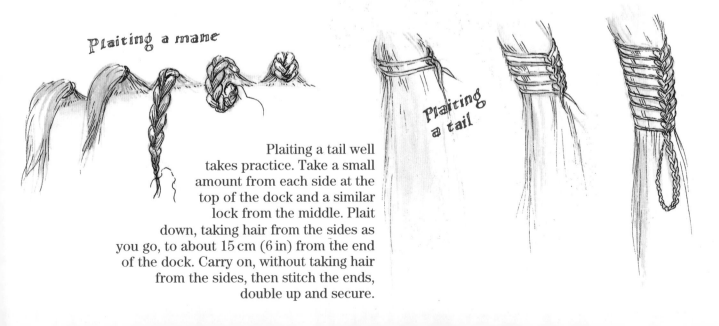

Plaiting a mane

Plaiting a tail

Plaiting a tail well takes practice. Take a small amount from each side at the top of the dock and a similar lock from the middle. Plait down, taking hair from the sides as you go, to about 15 cm (6 in) from the end of the dock. Carry on, without taking hair from the sides, then stitch the ends, double up and secure.

Choose a nice day to bath your pony and use a special horse shampoo (not detergent, it may irritate his skin). Use buckets of warm but not hot water if possible; on hot days use a hosepipe if he is not frightened of it. Wet the coat well before shampooing and rinse thoroughly. Walk him round to dry off so he does not catch cold.

If it is not warm enough for a full bath, just wash his mane and tail. Use buckets of water and shampoo as before, and stand to the side when washing his tail in case he tries to kick. It is difficult to plait newly washed hair, so if necessary wash him a couple of days before the show.

For local shows, you should wear a hat or skull cap, beige jodhpurs, jodhpur boots, shirt and tie, jacket and gloves. Long hair should be tied back or worn in a hairnet and you should carry the appropriate whip or showing cane. For cross-country, you need a skull cap, long-sleeved top, body protector, jodhpurs, jodhpur boots, gloves and whip.

Dress for Showing

Cross-country

To trim a tail, ask someone to hold an arm under the pony's dock to copy the natural angle at which the pony carries his tail on the move. Hold the ends of the tail hairs together and cut them straight across with a pair of scissors.

Make sure your tack is clean. Use saddle soap to clean the leather, but do not use shoe polish to try to get a shine because this makes the leather hard and slippery. Metalwork will shine if washed in hot water and dried immediately with a soft cloth.

It is always useful to have a waterproof rug to keep your pony dry and a waterproof coat to wear over your show clothes when it rains.

British Library Cataloguing in Publication Data
A catalogue record for this book is available from the British Library.

ISBN 0.85131.562.3

Published in Great Britain by
J.A. Allen & Company Ltd.,
1, Lower Grosvenor Place, Buckingham Palace Road,
London, SW1W 0EL.

Typeset in Hong Kong by Setrite Typesetters Ltd.
Printed in Hong Kong by Dah Hua Printing Press Co. Ltd.
Colour scanned in Hong Kong by Tenon & Polert Colour Scanning Ltd.